AUSCHWITZ LULLABY

A Play in Two Acts
by
JAMES C. WALL

Inspired by true events documented in the Auschwitz diaries of Dr. Miklos Nyiszli.

ST·OLAF
COLLEGE

Ex Munificentia
Robert Andrew Leraas
Interdisciplinary Studies Collection

Dramatic Publishing
Woodstock, Illinois • England • Australia • New Zealand

PS
3573
.A425S57
A87
2000

*** NOTICE ***

45154985

IMPORTANT BILLING AND CREDIT REQUIREMENTS

All producers of the play *must* give credit to the author(s) of the play in all programs distributed in connection with performances of the play and in all instances in which the title of the play appears for purposes of advertising, publicizing or otherwise exploiting the play and/or a production. The name of the author(s) *must* also appear on a separate line, on which no other name appears, immediately following the title, and *must* appear in size of type not less than fifty percent the size of the title type. *On all programs this notice should appear:*

"Produced by special arrangement with
THE DRAMATIC PUBLISHING COMPANY of Woodstock, Illinois"

* * * *

All producers of AUSCHWITZ LULLABY must include the following credit on the title page of all programs distributed in connection with performances of the play and on all advertising and promotional materials:

"This play was audio produced by Plays on Tape in 1999"

AUSCHWITZ LULLABY

A Drama in Two Acts
For 3 Men and 3 Women

CHARACTERS*

DR. ISAAC JONAH: Jewish Hungarian doctor of pathology, mid- to late 30s.

JACOB "CANADA" TANNENBAUM: Jewish prisoner who has been at Auschwitz for two years, mid- to late 20s.

CAPTAIN HANS GUNTER: A bureaucrat who runs Crematorium Number 2, mid- to late 30s.

KAPO EVA VACEK: Czech prisoner who works for the Germans, late 20s to early 30s.

MIRIAM JONAH: Wife of Dr. Jonah, mid- to late 30s.

LENA: Jewish girl, 16, who survives the gassing which murders her mother and father.

*More detailed character descriptions at end of playbook.

TIME and PLACE

September, 1944, Auschwitz-Birkenau concentration camp, Auschwitz, Poland. Act One encompasses the first three weeks Dr. Isaac Jonah is in the camp. Act Two is the beginning of the fourth week.

SET: The set should be suggestive more than realistic, with various areas of the stage used to show certain locations in and around Auschwitz concentration camp. A scrim might be used to back light shadows representing large numbers of soldiers and/or inmates.

The areas in the camp where action takes place:

1. The pathology laboratory: a dissecting table, a cabinet with medicines in it, a table with a stool at it and a microscope on it. Medicine bottles, specimens, books, typewriter.

2. The gas chamber of Crematorium Number 2: Indicated by a gross sculpture from hell, naked bodies are intertwined in a lattice-work mountain of bodies as the dying climbed over each other trying to reach the ceiling and air to breathe.

3. A room in the women's hospital; table and chair.

4. Dr. Isaac Jonah's room in the Sonderkommando barracks (center stage). This room is indicated by a single bed or cot, a small table with a chair or stool, and a sink or washstand.

5. Train ramp platform looking down on rail area where trains pull in with boxcars loaded with prisoners.

6. Area near front gate.

ACT ONE

SCENE ONE

AT RISE: *Darkness. Waltz music playing softly is heard. Then center stage a tight spotlight hits a figure standing in the darkness. DR. JONAH talks to the audience.*

enter on train ramps

JONAH. It is Tishri of the year 5705. My Christian friends call it late September of the year 1944. For the three weeks that I've been in this place, every night when I close my eyes, I can only see one thing. It's not my wife Miriam or my daughter Sarah. It's not my home or my laboratory. It's him, peering into a microscope, pretending for all the world like he's a scientist and that he knows what he's doing. *(He takes a scalpel from his coat pocket.)* The moment I shut my eyes, I dream I am standing behind him—like I do countless times each day since I was assigned to his lab. I grab the top of his head with my left hand— *(He uses his left hand and mimes grabbing the top of someone's head.)* —pull it back to expose the throat area and then with my right hand, I can *(He mimes slowly cutting someone's throat.)* feel the sharp blade penetrate the exterior and the interior carotid arteries. As I draw the scalpel through the left vertebral, my hand is dripping wet and blood is pumping now from the exterior and interior jugular veins. I pierce the larynx. I can feel blood droplets showering all over. He

7

resists and the gurgling sound from his throat is muffled when I cut through the phrenic and the vagus nerve—his respiratory system is shutting down. He is struggling less but I hold him tight and cut on through the trachea and then on to the right side jugular and carotids!

(CAPTAIN HANS GUNTER walks out onto the stage drawing his sidearm as he approaches JONAH.)

JONAH. I've opened a smile in his throat the size of a summer squash and he'll be dead within a minute. He has stopped struggling. The life is oozing out of him and I feel good! The body collapses onto the floor and I just stand here—waiting for—a guard, an officer—someone who will put the first bullet through my head...I die with a huge smile on my face... But they never come.

(GUNTER holsters his pistol and exits.)

JONAH. Because it is only a dream—I wish I was more courageous. I would do it and not care. But I have to care. Miriam and Sarah, next door in the women's camp. They're counting on me to care, to do something. Except, I'm scared. And I don't know what I can do. Three weeks we've been here. I feel totally helpless. All I have left is the fear that I may die at any moment. That's all that's left. Fear. From the moment we got off the train.

(Others appear out of the darkness at the sides of the stage making a kind of circle around JONAH: VACEK, GUNTER, CANADA, and lastly, Dr. Jonah's wife, MIRIAM; looking bewildered, she holds a suitcase.)

MIRIAM. Isaac, where are we?

JONAH. Auschwitz.

MIRIAM. What is this place?

JONAH. Hold on to Sarah... Put your hands over her ears... tighter!

MIRIAM (*mimes doing this to the unseen child in front of her*). Why are you trying to scare—

JONAH. Smell it?

MIRIAM. What?

JONAH. That sickening sweet smell. Everywhere... Burning flesh.

MIRIAM. What?

JONAH. This is a death camp!

(*MIRIAM retreats to the edges of the circle of light.*)

JONAH (*to the audience*). I know that killing is wrong. I am a doctor. Everything in my life—my profession, my religion, my upbringing, everything I believe tells me that killing is wrong. Yet I am consumed with thoughts of killing him: Josef Mengele, *Malach ha Mawis*— The Angel of Death.

(*VACEK comes into the light, addresses MIRIAM.*)

VACEK (*gesturing to the suitcase*). Put that over here with all the rest.

(*MIRIAM leaves the suitcase UC.*)

VACEK. Now get in line with everyone else. Hold on to your daughter there. She is certainly a pretty one, isn't she?

(GUNTER comes into the light. He stands on small platform.)

GUNTER. As you pass through the gates of Auschwitz, please notice the words above you. *"Arbeit Macht Frei."* Work Sets You Free! Everything's going to be fine. Follow everyone else to the end of the train ramp. Pay attention to Captain Mengele; he's the officer with the white gloves. He will tell you which line to go in: *Link* or *Recht*—Left or Right. Hurry up now. *Mach schnell.*

OFFSTAGE VOICE. *Link ... Link ... Link ... Recht ... Link ... Link ... Link.*

(CANADA comes forward. He opens a suitcase and starts to rifle through the contents as GUNTER walks by.)

GUNTER. Is there any suitcase that comes through Auschwitz that you don't get your filthy Jewish hands on?

CANADA. Captain Gunter, I'm assigned to the luggage. We're supposed to bring it into the camp and—

GUNTER. Not anymore! New postings this morning. You no longer work the train station ... You've been selected out!

(The look on CANADA's face shows he fears he's been "selected" to go to the gas chamber. GUNTER realizes he's thinking this.)

GUNTER. In the pit of your stomach, right? That sickly feeling that—my life might be coming to an end. *(Starts to walk away, pauses.)* Something to do with science classes in your background—you're the new orderly in Mengele's laboratory. *(He tears the star off CANADA's uniform.)* His help wear no stars... Not much you can organize from dead bodies, is there? *(He walks back to the edge of the light.)*

(CANADA and JONAH converse without looking at each other. CANADA rifles suitcase. JONAH puts on lab coat.)

JONAH. Who is that?

CANADA. Captain Gunter. He's in charge of Crematorium Number 2.

JONAH. How have you managed to survive this hell?

CANADA. I worked the trains.

JONAH. Was mine a good train? *(No answer from CANADA.)* People come here and die and you live off what you can steal from their possessions?

CANADA. In the Lager, "live" is to have more to eat than your ration of bread and watery soup. "Live" is one more shirt to ward off the freezing cold when winter comes and means death for hundreds all around you who don't have strength left to fight for their share of the food. They turn "Musslemen" and have maybe five, six days left to live. A few hours before they die, even the lice leave their bodies because there's nothing left to live off of. And the rest of us go on. Surviving for one more day, You string together as many of those days as you can, and that's what you call life.

JONAH. I didn't know.

Cross SLOff *(CANADA carries the suitcase back to the edge of the light.)*

OFFSTAGE VOICE. *Recht!*

JONAH. *Got! Ich vais nit vos tsu ton!*

OFFSTAGE VOICE. *Link!*   [Gunter]

JONAH. Give me a sign, God. Tell me what to do.

OFFSTAGE VOICE. *Recht!*

JONAH. Or at least let me wake up from this nightmare.

OFFSTAGE VOICE. *Link!*

JONAH. But all I hear is a voice at the end of the train ramp splitting everyone into two lines.

OFFSTAGE VOICE. *Recht!*

JONAH. And then Canada—damn him! Telling me what would have happened if ~~Miriam and Sarah~~ had gone to the left.
                                    I

OFFSTAGE VOICE. *Link!*

JONAH. The line ends with ~~their~~ my undressing.

OFFSTAGE VOICE. *Recht!*

JONAH. Sometimes in the courtyard, other times in the changing room.

OFFSTAGE VOICE. *Link!*

JONAH. The old, the sick, the crippled, young children clinging to their mothers, entire families.

(The light starts to grow dim.)

OFFSTAGE VOICE. *Recht!*

(GUNTER and VACEK stand near the edge of the light.)

VACEK. *Schnell! Schnell!* Hurry people. Hang up your clothes and please remember the number of the hook you've left them on. *(She exits.)*

GUNTER. Remember, after you've been showered and de-loused, report back to your assigning stations. Now move into the showers. *Schnell! Schnell! (As he watches people filing past him.)* Thank you... Thank you... Thank you... Guards! Count off as you leave the room! *(He exits.)*

OFFSTAGE VOICE. *Einz. Zwie. Drie. Fier. Fünf...*

(Lights go out. We hear heavy door clang shut. Silence, then the faint sound of waltz music mixed with crying, coughing, choking, and finally screaming. Then total silence.

SCENE TWO

AT RISE: *Darkness. We hear two voices: CANADA and DR. JONAH.*

CANADA. Dr. Jonah! Are you awake?

JONAH. Ah—yes—yes. What time is it, Canada?

CANADA. It'll be dawn soon. Come quickly. Bring your bag. We need you in the Number Two works. I can't believe it. This has never happened before.

JONAH. What are you talking about?

CANADA. In the gas chamber. One of them is still alive!

(Lights come up half on a shadowy form—a lattice-work mountain of dead, naked bodies, arms and legs inter-

*twined showing the struggle to get to the air near the
ceiling. JONAH with medical bag, CANADA with a
blanket enter, stop in horror. JONAH is frozen. CAN-
ADA moves to the far side, kneels over figure of a young
girl. He covers her with the blanket as the lights come
up more.)*

CANADA. God in Heaven! She is still alive!

JONAH. How?

CANADA. The floor is moist here. That means humidity.
Some gasses don't work well in humid conditions. And
her face is pressed into where the wall meets the floor—
maybe an air pocket. Doctor— *(Looks to JONAH who is
kneeling, praying.)* Doctor! What are we going to do?

JONAH. Let's get out of here!

CANADA. We can't!

JONAH. Where are the guards?

CANADA. They're still on break. You can't just leave her!
That's condemning her to death!

JONAH. No. The Germans already did that. This isn't
some nightmare in hell. This is real! Three thousand
Jews in here, all dead—except one! And they'll kill us
too if they find us in here.

CANADA. But we might be able to save her!

JONAH. Are you crazy? Think about what you are risking.

CANADA. I think—God meant for her to be saved.

JONAH. God? GOD?? I don't believe you! Look around us,
you damned fool! If God cared about any of us, would
this be happening?

*(CANADA gets JONAH's medical bag and rummages
through it.)*

JONAH. What are you doing?

CANADA. We've got to clear her lungs. What's in here that I can give her to make her sick it up? Jonah! What should I do?

JONAH. *Du gaist tsu schnell.* Slow down. I can't think. I'm too scared! *(He's come close enough to look down at her now.)* She's not even as old as my Sarah.

CANADA. Doctor—hurry!

JONAH *(kneels, gets a syringe, prepares it and gives her a shot).* What are you going to do with her?

CANADA. Bring her to the laboratory.

JONAH. And if someone sees us?

CANADA. You tell them she's one of Mengele's twins.

JONAH. Mengele! He's in and out of that lab ten times a day!

CANADA. Your room! We could hide her there!

JONAH. No! I'm not risking my life for—for someone—I don't even know!

CANADA *(picks her up and holds her close to him).* Two—years—I've been drowning in the smell of death. It's in my clothes, on my skin, even in my hair! But her hair—it smells like before! She's alive! She beat them! And maybe we can keep her alive a little longer! Your room, Jonah. It's the only chance we have. *(Beat.)* Hurry man! In seconds this place'll be swarming with guards! *(Still no answer from JONAH.)* Help me with her and I swear I'll do anything you ask—help you with anything, any time—you just—

JONAH. Teach me what I need to know to survive in this place—what my wife and daughter need to know to survive!

CANADA. And we can hide her in your room?

JONAH. Yes. But just until you can—

CANADA. Deal! Get your bag and check the hallway.

JONAH *(gets the bag, runs to side of stage, looks off, as he's praying).* "When we listen with our hearts, we can hear the lamentations through time's corridor..."

CANADA. Are you praying again?

JONAH. For the three weeks I've been here, I haven't stopped!

(JONAH signals OK, they exit, CANADA carrying the girl, JONAH with his medical bag as the lights go down and waltz music starts.)

SCENE THREE

AT RISE: *JONAH and MIRIAM meet center stage. She's been working with a garden hoe and is coming back inside the camp along with the crew she's been assigned to. JONAH has obviously been looking for her. He's searching, looking over each and every one of the unseen crew as they come back in through the gate. He reaches out to hold her. She drops the hoe.*

MIRIAM. Thank God you found us! Thank God! Thank God! My Isaac. My Isaac. *(She dissolves in to tears.)*

JONAH. Miriam! Miriam! Are you all right?

MIRIAM. Look at me, Isaac. They shaved my head.

JONAH. You look fine, Miriam. You look fine, do you hear me? *(He helps her up.)* Miriam, tell me—are you all right? How's Sarah? Where is she? *(He's looking at more of the unseen crew coming back inside the camp.)*

Is she on this detail with you? *(MIRIAM is still crying.)* Miriam! Please! We don't have much time.

(MIRIAM gets to her feet. CANADA comes on. He circles JONAH and MIRIAM. He sweeps for a time, then dries off newly washed beakers, test tubes, etc. Two realities mix here. His is the laboratory and he's teaching JONAH what he needs to know to survive but CANADA does not talk directly to JONAH nor do JONAH or MIRIAM respond or react to CANADA's words.)

CANADA. First you need to know someone—powerful, someone who can do you favors, someone who's probably been here a long time—doesn't matter if they're Jewish or German. To get this person to help you, you've got to have something you can do for them in return. What do you have to sell?

MIRIAM *(up now but still clinging to JONAH)*. I'm all right. My God. Isaac. I wasn't sure I'd ever see you again.

JONAH. Is Sarah with you?

MIRIAM. No. She's with some other girls her age—they're cleaning latrines and—God it's awful! *(She holds JONAH closely.)*

JONAH. Where do you go when you leave the camp?

MIRIAM. There's this farm. Rocks and weeds everywhere—my hands, look at the blisters. I don't know how to do things like— *(She points to the hoe on the ground.)*

CANADA. Every inmate is issued a food bowl. Take it with you everywhere—to the showers, the latrine, everywhere. If it's stolen, you won't eat for some time and that's always the beginning of the end.

JONAH. You have to learn! Whatever they tell you to do—learn it! Do it! And do it well, Miriam. You have to stay alive for Sarah. Remember, Sarah—can you do this?

MIRIAM. I'm scared, Isaac!

JONAH. I know, Miriam, I know. I am too.

MIRIAM. I want to go home! Remember the apple tree in our backyard? And the gazebo. You were going to paint the gazebo when summer was over before the leaves started to fall. Remember?

JONAH. I know. I'm sorry. The time just—

MIRIAM. Was it just a month ago? We were sitting outside, after dinner—and you were saying that—

JONAH (bringing MIRIAM back to reality). Miriam! Do you get enough to eat, where you are? Because I'm a pathologist, they put me to work in Mengele's lab. I have my own small room and food.

MIRIAM (encouraged by this). Who is this Mengele? Can he help us?

CANADA. At night, the smart inmate can tell when the piss pot is too near the top. That's when you hold it in, no matter what. The last person to piss when it reaches the top of the bucket, the guard makes you empty it. That costs you precious moments of sleep and steals away the strength you need to survive.

JONAH. He's a madman. He thinks he's a scientist but he's not. He has these insane theories he's trying to prove—and all the human guinea pigs he could ever possibly want.

MIRIAM. What does he have you do?

JONAH. Autopsies. That's all—so far. Watch over Sarah.

(VACEK comes on, picks up the hoe.)

VACEK. Even if your husband is Mengele's new Jew doctor, you still have to report for roll call. *(She takes MIRIAM's hands in hers.)* Someone has seen fit to change your work assignment. Yes, yes. I can see why. No. These hands weren't meant for farming. Tomorrow you will be assigned to me in the women's hospital.

(JONAH and his wife are overjoyed.)

MIRIAM. The women's hospital, Isaac. Did you hear that?

JONAH. Thank you, Kapo. Thank you. My daughter Sarah. Do you think she could—

VACEK. The one with the lovely brown eyes? She's one of my favorites. I'll watch over her, don't you worry. Such a beautiful family you have, Doctor.

CANADA. More than anything else, though—the single most important thing you need to survive in the lager— is shoes! Treasure them. Guard them. Care for them. Because without them, sooner or later, you won't be able to work. And when that moment comes, they have no use for you anymore ... You're dead.

VACEK. Roll call. *Schnell!*

JONAH. Miriam. We're going to survive this, do you hear me? Be strong! I love you; don't ever forget that! Be strong for Sarah!

(MIRIAM starts to exit, stops and looks back at JONAH.)

JONAH. And Miriam—tell your barber—not so short on the sides, next time, OK?

(They try to laugh bravely as MIRIAM exits. VACEK is holding the hoe upside down. She playfully shoves the handle end between JONAH's legs, down by his ankles. She moves it up a bit, suggestively. She looks off in the direction MIRIAM has gone.)

VACEK. No offense, Judah, but I've seen thousands like her. She won't last a month. If you decide you want a woman—whenever—I can arrange things.

(JONAH stares at her hatefully for a moment and she walks off as lights go down and waltz music is heard.)

SCENE FOUR

SCENE: *Jonah's room in the barracks. There's a small bed, table, chair, perhaps some type of wash basin or sink.*

AT RISE: *LENA is asleep on bed under the blankets. JONAH puts away letter he was writing as she starts to wake.*

LENA *(half asleep)*. Poppa. Hold me, Poppa. Where's Momma? I don't see Momma anywhere.
JONAH. Shhh! *Shtil, mayn kind.* Someone will hear you.
LENA *(sits up, looks around)*. Who are you?
JONAH. I am a doctor. My name is Isaac Jonah.
LENA. Where am I?
JONAH. This is my room, here in the camp where they brought you. What is your name?

LENA. Lena.

JONAH. How old are you, Lena?

LENA. Sixteen. *(She realizes she is wearing strange clothes.)* What is this?

JONAH. It's one of my shirts. How do you feel?

LENA. Not so good. Where are my clothes?

JONAH. Don't worry about that now. You've been through quite a lot.

LENA. Where are my mother and father? Are they with another doctor, like you?

JONAH. Why don't you lie back and I'll give you something to help you rest, would you like that?

LENA. Momma and Poppa. Where are they?

JONAH. Shhh. Close your eyes, Lena, and just—

LENA. I want to know where they are!

JONAH. Your parents are gone, child. I'm sorry.

LENA. What do you mean?

JONAH. No one can hurt them anymore. They are with God now.

LENA. I don't believe you. I have to go find them!

JONAH. You can't.

LENA. Get my clothes, please. I have to go look for my parents. They're alive. I know they are. You're wrong. Why would you— *(Frightened that someone will hear, JONAH approaches the bed.)* Don't you get near me! I'm leaving here. I've got to look for—

JONAH *(restraining her)*. Be still! Listen to me! If you try to leave here, the soldiers will find you and they'll kill you. And then they'll kill me for just having you in here! Do you understand? They'll kill us both—just like they did your poor mother and father!

LENA. I don't believe you!

(CANADA hurries in. He's carrying one or two large medical books.)

CANADA. Not so loud! You can be heard all the way down the hall!

JONAH. Was anyone out there?

LENA. Who is he?

CANADA. I ran into Rhodes. I told him you needed these brought to your room. I don't think anyone heard. *(To LENA.)* My name is Jacob. You can call me Canada. I'm a friend.

LENA. Can you take me to my parents?

JONAH. Her name is Lena. She won't believe me.

CANADA. Lena—how much do you remember—about arriving here at the camp?

LENA *(starts out slowly)*. I remember a lot of noises—dogs barking and soldiers shouting. And I was singing—softly—to myself. Sometimes—when I'm afraid... But—wait—yes, there was a waltz—a Strauss waltz. I remember now. But then— *(She closes her eyes and covers her ears.)* Coughing, and choking, and— I remember a hand in front of my face. And a ring. I was trying to remember something about that ring.

CANADA *(takes a ring from his pocket)*. Is this the ring?

LENA. It's Momma's.

CANADA. She was on top of you. Trying to cover you.

LENA. Momma.

CANADA. Your face was pressed against the wall. You were shielded—not only by—

LENA. Poppa.

CANADA. Somehow there was an air pocket. You never got the full effect of the gas.

LENA. They're dead! Oh, Momma! Poppa! I'm scared. *(She breaks down in to tears. JONAH comforts her.)*

JONAH. It's over, Lena. You're safe now. Go ahead and cry. Go right ahead.

LENA *(sees the syringe JONAH has prepared for her)*. What is that?

JONAH *(giving her the shot)*. This will help you sleep. Lie back down, Lena, and close your eyes.

LENA. You're a very brave man.

JONAH. What?

LENA. Thank you for saving me.

JONAH. Close your eyes. *(He sits on a stool near the bed and sings her the refrain from the lullaby "Roshenkis Mit Mandlen." Note: See back of book for melody.) "Yideles wiegele. Shteit a klohr weiss Tziegele Dos tziegele is geforen handlen Dos vet sein dein beruf Roshenkis Mit Mandlin Shluf sie Yidele shluf." (LENA is asleep now.)*

CANADA. "Raisins and Almonds." I haven't thought of that song in years.

JONAH. I used to sing it to my Sarah. She swore she always woke up hungry the next morning... She's going to need some food. And some clothes. Do you have anything for her to wear?

CANADA. I'm working on it.

JONAH. For God's sake, what are you going to do with her?

CANADA. Try to keep her alive for the time being.

JONAH. What do you think you can do for her, except put off the inevitable?

CANADA. Life is incredibly cheap here. You learn fast, Doctor.

JONAH. My wife, my child—if something I do puts their lives in jeopardy—

CANADA. I know about your responsibilities.

JONAH. Why are you risking so much?

CANADA. In the two years I've been here, hundreds of thousands have done the dance of death. *(Shakes his head.)* Not her!

JONAH. That's the first time I've had to tell anyone— something like that.

CANADA. She reminds you of your own daughter, doesn't she?

JONAH. There is much more to you, Jacob Tannenbaum, than just surviving and organizing. Why do they call you "Canada"?

CANADA. The Nazi storehouse for the gold and the valuables—the Polish Jews called it "Canada," their idea of a place of wealth and prosperity. Because of my talents, the name became mine too.

JONAH. Do you think we could get her into the women's camp?

CANADA. It's possible, but it's risky.

JONAH. Just get her out of here as quickly as you can.

CANADA. Even if we could get her into the women's camp, she's not automatically safe.

JONAH. Who would notice one more among thousands of—

CANADA. The Germans would. They take roll call twice a day. They love the adding and the subtracting, the counting and recounting. We know there's a train scheduled to leave here tomorrow night with two hundred women volunteers for a factory north of here. If we could somehow get Lena on that train, that would be the first step to freedom. *(He sits near the bed and sings some of the English version of* "Roshenkis Mit Mandlen.") "The goat will trot to the market, While mother her watch will keep, To bring you back raisins and almonds, Sleep, my little one, sleep."

(GUNTER enters, bottle in hand, a little drunk.)

GUNTER. What is this? A choir practice in— *(He stops, seeing CANADA, who moves to block sight of LENA.)*

JONAH. Good evening, Captain.

CANADA. Good evening, sir.

GUNTER. Good evening to you, Jew doctor. *(Pointing to CANADA.)* Why is he in your room? *(He sees LENA lying on the bed.)* Who is that? *(He walks closer to bed.)* I said—who is that in your bed, Doctor? *(He's reaching out to lift the blanket to see her better.)*

CANADA. She's an experiment.

GUNTER *(to CANADA).* Silence! *(To JONAH.)* I asked you, Doctor.

JONAH. She is a twin. Dr. Mengele wanted her observed to see if there was any kind of reaction between twins even when separated by some distance.

GUNTER. Reaction to what?

JONAH. Certain—stimuli.

GUNTER. Hah! I can imagine! Get her out of here.

JONAH. Canada, you may take her back to the lab now if you would.

(CANADA carries LENA in blanket and exits.)

GUNTER *(looking around Jonah's room)*. How does it feel being the only Jew in Eastern Europe to have such luxurious living quarters? Even a window. Do you like the view? *(No answer from JONAH.)* Please, please. Sit, Herr Doctor. *(JONAH sits on his bed.)* Do you play chess?

JONAH. Yes.

GUNTER. We will play sometime... How does your wife like her new work assignment?

JONAH. You?

GUNTER *(nods his head, looks out the window)*. It's cold for a September night. Going to be a bad winter... The moon is up—look at all the stars—

JONAH. Is there something I can help you with?

GUNTER *(ignoring his question)*. Of all the branches of medicine—you chose pathology. Not very exciting. Why is that?

JONAH. My papa died when I was very young. The doctors didn't know why. I wanted to look for answers—not the easy ones on the surface, but—inside.

GUNTER *(nodding his head)*. Looking for answers... I can see that. I wanted to go to medical school once. I could have been a doctor.

JONAH. What happened?

GUNTER. My family couldn't afford to send me.

JONAH. Is this why you hate Jews?

GUNTER. The Zionist conspiracy to control all the wealth in our world cost me my dream. *(Takes another drink.)* You of course deny that such a conspiracy exists or that you are responsible for any of it, right?

JONAH. Getting Sarah to eat her cabbage is the only conspiracy my wife and I—

GUNTER. Everything about you is different: your foods, your traditions, even your God.

JONAH. I didn't know my God was different from yours.

GUNTER. You hate Christians.

JONAH. Isn't the message of the Torah and your gospels much the same?

GUNTER. Which is?

JONAH. Love your neighbor as you love the Lord.

GUNTER. So now it's "Matthew, Mark, Luke, and Jonah"? *(Silence for a moment.)* Before the war I was an office manager for a small manufacturing firm.

JONAH. What happened to your arm?

GUNTER. A clumsy accident on our loading dock. Kept me out of active service. But my managerial skills are perfect for camp work.

JONAH. So you kill people.

GUNTER. I run a crematorium where bodies are disposed of. I volunteered to serve because I want to make something of my life.

JONAH. You still believe in this war?

GUNTER. In the Third Reich? No, of course not. I'm not a stupid man, Doctor.

JONAH. Then why are you—

GUNTER *(takes a long swig from the bottle and pulls a chair up near the bed where JONAH is sitting).* Do you consider yourself courageous?

JONAH. I don't know.

GUNTER. Do you think killing is wrong?

JONAH. I believe it is.

(GUNTER takes his Luger pistol out of its holster and puts it to the side of JONAH's head. JONAH closes his

eyes, waiting for the end. GUNTER laughs, and lays it carefully on the bed next to JONAH. JONAH, his eyes now open, watches as he does this and just stares at the pistol. GUNTER rises, walks to the window, mimes opening it and turns to JONAH.)

GUNTER. Can you smell the death, Doctor? Doesn't your heart cry out for vengeance? *(Pointing to the weapon.)* Go on. Shoot me. *(GUNTER offers himself as a target. JONAH looks at the gun, reaches out for it, hesitates, stops and then turns away.)* I guess we know how courageous you are. *(GUNTER reholsters his pistol. He takes a long look out the window.)* When you requisition medicines for your lab, will you be needing any morphine?

JONAH. Some form of opiate drug might be needed in the course of—

GUNTER. Get more than you'll actually need. *(Takes another long drink from his bottle.)*

JONAH. Your arm? *(GUNTER nods.)* They're your storehouses. You're an officer. You don't need my help to get—

GUNTER. Everything is controlled—counted and signed for.

JONAH. I want to see my wife and daughter—every day.

GUNTER. You are in no position to—

JONAH. I'm going to die, aren't I? If not today or tomorrow, then next week or next month!

GUNTER *(stares out the window as he considers the risk).* Two people leaving the women's camp—questions will be asked... One. That is not quite as risky. Choose which one.

JONAH *(takes a moment to make this painful decision).* My wife.

GUNTER *(stepping back from the window).* Look out your window, Doctor. What do you see?

JONAH *(looking out the window).* It looks like it's snowing. *(GUNTER reaches out and catches something on his fingertips, draws his hand back inside and holds it out to JONAH.)* Ashes!

GUNTER *(smearing some ash on JONAH's face).* Jews!! *(He wipes his fingers clean.)* Tomorrow you will requisition morphine, yes? *(JONAH nods. GUNTER hands JONAH the almost-empty bottle.)* Would you care for some schnapps, Doctor?

(Lights go down as waltz music comes up.)

SCENE FIVE

AT RISE: *Downstage, MIRIAM sits at a small table. She is in a very small room in the women's hospital. On the table are heaps of white cloth. She is cutting out material to be used as diapers. VACEK enters, picks up a clipboard, examines the diapers MIRIAM has finished, folds them, and stashes them away.*

VACEK. How do you like cutting out diapers?

MIRIAM. If it's for the children, I don't mind.

VACEK. Do you believe what they say—pregnant women have a special beauty?

MIRIAM. When I was with Sarah, I was as big as a house. That's not beautiful!

VACEK. My husband, Horst, and I have only one child. Anton is four, the apple of his father's eye. You're very lucky: a beautiful daughter, a faithful husband. Is he always faithful?

MIRIAM. Isaac? *(Laughing)* You don't know my husband. He's as faithful as an old shoe.

VACEK. It was probably nothing. Except, the other day when you went off to roll call, I thought he was hinting that he wouldn't mind meeting some other women prisoners... "Jonah"—that certainly doesn't sound Jewish.

MIRIAM. My husband's father changed it.

VACEK. Trying to hide your identity?

MIRIAM. It was long ago. He was a religious man. And he loved fishing.

VACEK. I like to study people's names. The orphanage sent me to so many families, I can't remember how many names I've had.

MIRIAM. You grew up in an orphanage?

VACEK. Don't say it like it's a dirty word. The Sisters of the Holy Infant. They have an orphanage with their convent in a small town just outside of Prague.

MIRIAM. I suppose finding homes for little children—

VACEK *(lying)*. Oh there were many homes. They just could never find the right one for me. Either they already had children who became jealous of me after a while. Or if I was the only child, they'd spoil me shamelessly and the Sisters would snatch me back to—

MIRIAM. How long were you there?

VACEK. Till I was grown. I was going to take vows—become a nun.

MIRIAM. What happened?

VACEK. God sent me a sign... Where in Hungary did you come from?

MIRIAM. Budapest.

VACEK. And what was it like there?

MIRIAM. It was beautiful. My parents have a farm a mile outside of town. We'd take Sarah there on Sundays and she'd play in the fields.

VACEK. The Sisters owned a large farm behind the convent. And there were gardens and a lake we swam in during the summer. My favorite place was a grotto, a shrine to the Holy Family. I would stop there every day when I was out walking and kneel and say a prayer.

MIRIAM. Were your prayers ever answered?

VACEK. You're a Jew! What would you know about prayers?

MIRIAM. My people were praying centuries before— *(She stops, realizing the danger of her anger. There's silence between them for a moment.)* We had such a beautiful yard. We had trees and a garden. Isaac promised me this summer that he was finally going to get the gazebo painted. Sarah just loves to play in that gazebo.

VACEK. What does the name "Miriam" mean?

MIRIAM. One who rebels.

VACEK *(laughing)*. You people are so amusing... How is your daughter Sarah?

MIRIAM. I worry about her so much.

VACEK. I've decided I'm going to adopt her.

MIRIAM. What?

VACEK. Growing up as I did, I know what happens when you don't have parents in your life who love you and watch over you.

MIRIAM. I love Sarah! I—watch—over her!

VACEK. Oh, of course. But for how much longer?

(She is standing behind MIRIAM. She reaches in front of her and draws her finger across MIRIAM's throat as if cutting her throat. Lights go out as waltz music comes up.)

SCENE SIX

SCENE: *Pathology lab.*

AT RISE: *Lena is wrapped in blanket and asleep on dissecting table. CANADA packs small parcels into a large box. JONAH enters.*

CANADA. Dr. Jonah. Are you all right?
JONAH. Gunter was drunk. I thought for sure he was going to kill me.
CANADA. What did he want?
JONAH. To scare me. He wants morphine for his arm.
CANADA. Morphine!
JONAH. He's an addict, or very close to it.
CANADA. Good! We can use this.
JONAH. How?
CANADA. Blackmail him. Once you start giving him the morphine, we'll keep a record of how much and how often.
JONAH. So you know a nasty little secret about an officer?
CANADA. He's serious about his career; that's all we need. This could mean arms, ammunition—even help, maybe, in getting her out.

JONAH. Gunter?

CANADA. He works the train ramp. They all pull that duty in rotation. And he knows about the schedules.

JONAH. So I'll just say: Captain Gunter, I've kept a record of how many cc's of morphine I've stolen for you and now I'd like some bullets, some pistols—and, oh yes— Please—Let My People Go! And Gunter looks at this Moses of medicine and puts a bullet in my head! No thank you, my friend. This is one Hungarian Jew who wants to stay alive.

CANADA *(laughing).* "Moses of Medicine." That's good, Doctor. I like that.

(They both start to laugh, and it almost gets to the point where the sound of the laughter causes them to laugh more. JONAH stops.)

JONAH. Oh! I'm sorry. We shouldn't be laughing—not like that, not here.

CANADA. Doctor—once you forget how to laugh, you forget how to live. Besides, isn't that what being "The Chosen People" means? We laugh and cry better than anyone else.

(LENA wakes. CANADA brings her the clothes they have for her.)

JONAH. How do you feel, Lena?

LENA. Hungry. It is morning or nighttime?

JONAH. It's late at night.

CANADA. I found some clothes for you. I'm sorry; it's the best we could do.

LENA *(taking clothes from him).* Where can I—

CANADA. You can dress in the storeroom. It's a bit drafty, but it's private enough. *(CANADA helps her down from the table, ushers her to storeroom.)* We'll be out here working. Before you come out, Lena, make certain it's just our two voices you hear, understand?

LENA. I think so, yes. Thank you.

(She exits. JONAH and CANADA continue taping shut and putting address labels on the boxes.)

JONAH. Canada, about your plan. I've never been a fighter. But if I fight for anything, Miriam and Sarah come first.

CANADA. I understand.

JONAH. You have my word. I won't say anything to betray you. I do hope you succeed.

CANADA. In the Lager, I have met German Jews, Hungarian Jews, Czech Jews. Even Italian Jews and Greek Jews from Salonica. All those other names come first, then "Jew" second. As if the first word—the German, the Polish, the Hungarian—apologizes for the "Jew" that follows. *(JONAH turns to protest.)* Oh, I know. I do it myself. We all do—except the Nazis! They don't care. We're all one to them.

(They work in silence for a moment.)

JONAH *(looking at a table with assorted bottles of chemicals on it).* The supplies we ordered?

CANADA. Everything should be there.

JONAH. Evipol, chloroform, yes—this is fine. Mengele wants us to get these boxes ready for Berlin.

CANADA. What is all this we're shipping out?

JONAH. Body parts. Preserved in formaldehyde... Can you teach me—how to live with the guilt?

CANADA. Guilt?

JONAH. For being alive.

CANADA. There was an old man, a doctor. He was from Munich like me. He knew a lot of my grandfather's friends. Rosen was his name. We became friends my first month here. We used to talk about medicine sometimes. It was a way of staying sane. He made me promise him that once the war was over, I'd go to medical school and become a doctor. That last morning, before they took him away, I asked him how he was feeling. He said: "I could use a month's rest in the country. This Auschwitz place doesn't agree with me so much."

JONAH. You loved him, didn't you?

CANADA. He reminded me so much of my father. Except that my father hated doctors. Rosen said if a friend is killed and you can do something, and you don't, you have guilt to live with. But if you go down to the root cellar for a potato and come out and find the whole world has gone crazy, don't go crazy blaming yourself. You didn't do this. So, you do what you can. How much is that, I asked. He said—each man has to decide that for himself. *(Beat.)* I'm going to check on the girl.

JONAH. She's going to be famished. I might be able to get into the kitchen. I'll see what I can find for her to eat. Be careful. Hopefully, this late no one will—

CANADA. Go for the food. I'll watch things here.

(JONAH exits. CANADA continues taping boxes and then suddenly VACEK enters from side opposite where JONAH exited.)

VACEK. Why are there lights on in here? What are you doing?

CANADA *(nervously eyeing the supply room door)*. These specimens—Dr. Mengele decided late this afternoon he wants them packaged and ready to ship to Berlin early tomorrow. *(VACEK looks around the lab.)* Is there something I could help you with?

VACEK. How do you survive now, Canada? No trains, no suitcases—no more organizing. *(No answer from CANADA.)* I understand you've found a new family for yourself with the Jew doctor in this laboratory of death. *(She picks up a few things and examines them.)* They're watching dirty movies in the officers' mess. Most of them are drunk tonight. *(She circles CANADA, reaching out touching his hand or his arm. He tries not to react, stealing glances towards where LENA exited.)* Sometimes, when they're showing the sex movies, I sneak into their special kitchen. There's a pass-through to the dining room; the doors don't close all the way. I watch the movies. Canada, do you think I'm as attractive as the women in those films? *(No answer from CANADA.)* The last time I slept with a man—an officer—he whispered across my pillow that I had a beautifully plain face. As if you can be so plain, that it somehow becomes beautiful. What would you whisper across my pillow, Canada?

CANADA. Where I sleep, there are no pillows.

VACEK. If I took off every stitch of clothing I have on— would you take me?

CANADA. No.

VACEK. Why not?

CANADA *(wrapping a carton)*. You're a Kapo.

VACEK. So you hate me.

CANADA. Didn't you know? It's a camp rule.

VACEK. Always with the jokes.

CANADA. Don't you find it curious? I mean, the irony of a German war meant to cleanse the world of inferior humanity, a war that lets out of the woodwork sadists and sociopaths and garbage like you! *(Rather than being angry, VACEK gets excited by the insults.)* Somebody once told me that you had a choice between going in to a convent or going to bed with the devil. And you chose the devil.

VACEK *(getting close to CANADA)*. Did you ever think— maybe he chose me? *(We hear a sneeze offstage.)* What was that? *(She moves in the direction of the supply room off the lab.)*

CANADA. What was what?

VACEK *(moves toward supply room)*. Come out of there! *Schnell!*

(LENA comes out, walking very slowly, obviously scared. VACEK grabs her.)

VACEK. Who is this?

CANADA. She's one of Mengele's patients.

VACEK. You're lying! She was hiding in there!

CANADA. No, she wasn't.

VACEK *(turns LENA around so she can get a good look at her)*. My, you are a pretty one, aren't you? *(Beat.)* You look like a dancer! Have you ever danced a waltz? *(No answer from the frightened LENA.)* Come dance with me.

(She takes LENA by both hands and starts to dance a slow circling waltz with her, humming some waltz music. VACEK is obviously enthralled with LENA and totally forgets about CANADA. LENA is getting more and more frightened. CANADA tries to take LENA away from VACEK.)

CANADA. Stop this! I tell you Dr. Mengele is going to be—

VACEK *(grabbing a scalpel and holding it to LENA's throat)*. Who is she?

CANADA. I already told you. She's one of Mengele's—

VACEK *(to LENA, leaning in very close)*. Are you from Uncle Pepi's zoo? Has he offered you a ride in his car? He'll say "Let's play a game called chimney!" Have you ever played with the Angel of Death?

CANADA *(moving towards VACEK)*. She's here because she's a twin!

VACEK. Where's the other one?

CANADA. With Mengele.

(Unseen by VACEK, JONAH returns.)

VACEK *(holding LENA tightly, scalpel close to her neck)*. He's lying, little girl. And lying is a sin. When someone lies, someone has to wipe the slate clean. I'm afraid, pretty little girl, that you're that someone. Now this isn't really going to hurt—

CANADA. All right! She's Dr. Jonah's daughter.

VACEK. His daughter? How many daughters does he have? I know the one— *(She stops to think for a moment.)* Where is he?

CANADA. I have no idea.

VACEK. Go find him and bring him here. I can wait. Maybe this is his daughter, and maybe it isn't. He'll tell me. I hope it is. You know, I've never taken a little girl while her own father watched me do it. What do you think about that, Jewboy?

(VACEK's hand comes down from LENA's mouth. The girl is sobbing. VACEK holds scalpel to LENA's throat with one hand; with the other she starts to pull down the top of the girl's dress to expose her breasts. JONAH has put down tray of food. He quietly picks up bottle of chloroform, uncorks it, puts some on his handkerchief, and from behind reaches in front of VACEK, covering her mouth and nose. LENA runs to CANADA who holds her. VACEK struggles for a moment and then goes limp as JONAH lets her down to the floor. They all stand there for a moment looking at VACEK on the floor.)

CANADA *(to JONAH)*. She saw me. She saw Lena!

JONAH. I know.

CANADA *(grabbing the scalpel)*. We have to kill her!

JONAH. No!

CANADA. But she knows! She'll wake up and she'll run to the first German officer she sees and—

JONAH. Canada—NO!

CANADA. She is a monster!

JONAH. So you should become one too? *(Beat.)* Leave Vacek to me. You concentrate on getting Lena out of this place! I am going to help you any way I can! Do you hear me, Canada? In any way! *(He puts his arms around LENA; CANADA joins them.)* We're going to get you out of here, Lena. Don't be afraid of anything. You are safe now, I promise you!

CANADA. Thank you "Moses." Thank you!

(Lights; curtain.)

END OF ACT ONE

ACT TWO

SCENE ONE

SCENE: *Dr. Jonah's room.*

AT RISE: *LENA is standing, looking out a window.*

LENA *(singing)*. "I have a little *dreidel*, I made it out of clay. And when it's dry and ready, Then *dreidel* I shall play"—

JONAH *(returning to his room, shaving things in hand)*. Lena! Shhhhhhh! Someone might hear. I'm sorry. Please move away from the window. We have to be very careful.

LENA. I haven't sung that song in years. The sun coming up—reminded me of when— *(Her voice trails off.)*

JONAH. I remember. Sarah used to sing it when she was little. *Dreidels* were her favorite toy. She'd spin them and spin them— *(He puts food down on the cot.)* Here. Sit down and eat some of this. How do you feel?

LENA *(sitting and eating)*. My head feels heavy.

JONAH. That will clear.

LENA. I don't usually have sausage for breakfast.

JONAH. Eat slowly and chew your food.

LENA. You sound just like my poppa. He sings to me before I go to sleep.

JONAH. He sounds like a fine man.

LENA. You gave me a shot of something.

JONAH. Evipol, a sleeping drug. So—do you like school?

LENA. Besides music, my favorite subject is mathematics.

JONAH. Good for you. My daughter Sarah is not so good with numbers but she likes music—and boys! If only she'd stop talking with the boys and pay more attention to her schoolwork.

LENA. Does Sarah have boyfriends? I do!

JONAH. You do?

LENA. Of course. Don't you think I'm pretty enough?

JONAH. Oh yes! I do. Is there a special one?

LENA. There was this boy named Marcus. He carried my books after school. But when we got to the front gate, my mother was pruning some bushes and she saw us. She said I was much too young to be turning boys' heads. *(She looks around the room and her happy expression changes to one of sorrow.)*

JONAH. We're going to try to get you out of here.

LENA. How?

JONAH. Canada and his friends are working on it. Now, finish your breakfast. What happened with this boy Marcus?

LENA. I don't like him anymore! And I don't like sausages for breakfast! What difference will it make if I die hungry or not?

JONAH. Lena, you mustn't say things like that.

LENA. But my mother, my father—

JONAH. But you're alive! That's what matters now. A train is leaving here tonight. If we can get you on it, you'll go to a real work camp. I don't know the details, but you'll be alive and maybe have a chance someday to be free!

LENA. And then what? Even if I could find my way there, I can't go home. No one's left. They were all on the train!

JONAH. You have to have faith in yourself. Even when your fear is so big, it's swallowed you up whole and all around you it's dark and strange and you don't know what to do—that's when you have to believe in yourself—and especially in God.

LENA. I'm afraid.

JONAH. Pray to God. He'll help you find the courage— *(Touching his chest.)* in here. God will help you find the courage you have inside of you.

LENA. How many people have died here?

JONAH. I don't know.

LENA. In the time you've been here?

JONAH. Maybe ten thousand.

LENA. You say it so simply.

JONAH. "Ten thousand people." I don't know how else to say it.

LENA. Three words take in all those lives!

JONAH. How CAN you say it? They're stripped naked, gassed, and then burned. If I say it for each one— *(He stops, realizing he shouldn't be talking about this to her.)* I'm sorry, Lena. You shouldn't bother yourself with—

LENA. So many have died. And some live. Why is that?

JONAH. They need people to work.

LENA. You make it sound so casual. People working, like nothing is happening out there, like it's a game that you've won.

JONAH. This isn't a game and we've won nothing! You try to get from one hour to the next. Night comes and you're so worn out from the fear, you'd think it'd be easy to sleep. But the nights are the worst time of all.

LENA. Why?

JONAH. Last night, I dreamed I'd escaped. I was far, far away from here and the air was clean and smelled so good. It was snowing. The most beautiful snow I'd ever seen. But it wouldn't stop. It kept falling and falling. An eternity of snow! Soon I was being buried alive and— *(Again he stops when he realizes she shouldn't hear this.)*

LENA. What happened?

JONAH. Nothing. It was a nightmare. That's all.

LENA. I don't think I've ever had a nightmare.

JONAH. You should only have good dreams.

LENA. Most of the time I do.

JONAH. Tell me the happiest one you can remember.

LENA *(a little embarrassed)*. It was about Marcus. Do you really want to hear?

JONAH. I think so.

LENA. Does Sarah ever go to the cinema?

JONAH. Of course.

LENA. Do she and her boyfriend ever sit in the balcony?

JONAH. Maybe I shouldn't hear this.

LENA. Sarah does date, doesn't she?

JONAH. Not yet. And after this conversation, maybe never. *(Beat.)* Maybe when this insane war is over and we're all out of here and free—maybe I'll allow her to go with you and your boyfriend— *(He nods.)* the four of you. Yes, I think so.

LENA. Oh could we? Please? Could we go to the cinema?

JONAH. On one condition.

LENA. I know— No balcony! No kissing!

JONAH. Except maybe in your dreams. *(Beat.)* I have to go to the laboratory now. You're going to have to hide in here the rest of the day. Keep away from the window and the door. Stay in the bed and if you hear someone, cover yourself with the blanket. Will you be all right?

LENA. I think so.

JONAH. Try to rest. I'll bring you some food around lunch time. *(He starts to exit.)*

LENA. Dr. Isaac. *(He turns back to her. LENA is up out of the bed. She crosses to him and hugs him with all her might.)* Thank you. Thank you. *(At first he doesn't know how to react and then he hugs her back.)*

JONAH. You're welcome, child. You are so welcome!

(JONAH exits. Lights go down as waltz music is heard.)

SCENE TWO

SCENE: *The workroom in the women's hospital.*

AT RISE: *Later the same day. Lights up. VACEK is sitting in a small tub of water. She is bare-breasted or perhaps wearing a light, sleeveless T-shirt. MIRIAM enters carrying a bucket of warm water, towels, and a sponge. VACEK eats an apple as MIRIAM gives her a sponge bath.*

VACEK. I love apples. Have you ever noticed? The skin is like a woman's skin. You polish the outside—the more you caress it, the better the inside tastes. *(Beat.)* Are you embarrassed to touch another woman?

MIRIAM. I do what I am told.

VACEK. Why?

MIRIAM. To stay alive. To help my Sarah stay alive.

VACEK. How many daughters do you have?

MIRIAM. One.

VACEK. And you'd do just about anything for her, wouldn't you? *(No answer from MIRIAM.)* Don't depend on your doctor husband. He works for Mengele. Mengele puts to death more people in one day than you or I can imagine.

MIRIAM. Why are you trying to scare me?

VACEK. Your husband has already asked for a woman in his room.

MIRIAM. I don't believe you.

VACEK. Suit yourself. *(She smells her arms and her shoulders.)* Wash my back again. I can still smell the whiskey everywhere. I suppose everyone's talking about this? *(No answer from MIRIAM.)* Have you heard your kike friends talking about this?

MIRIAM. No, I haven't.

VACEK. They say I was drunk. Lying there in the garbage cans outside the officers' mess. Someone had poured whiskey all over me. I stunk to high hell of it. No one believed me when I told them what had really happened. I was in your husband's laboratory. His thieving assistant Canada was there and he saw—I know he saw. He's avoided me so far today but when I catch up with him— I'll find out who it was. *(She takes bite of her apple and is pleased with how good it tastes.)* Ummmmmmmm! Someone's going to die. *(She starts to giggle at the thought of it, how pleasing it is.)*

MIRIAM *(stands back, a little defiant, not as scared as before)*. Who are you?

VACEK *(amused at being questioned by a prisoner)*. I'm a Kapo, my little rebel.

MIRIAM. You're not a Nazi. You're not a German. Why do you hurt people?

VACEK. I was arrested and brought here—like all of you. The Germans need someone to dirty their fingers touching what they won't. That's what I do. I touch all the dirty things.

MIRIAM. I don't know whether to pity you—or just hate you!

VACEK *(pointing to the inside of her right thigh)*. Do you have a mole—right there, on the inside of your thigh—like Sarah does? *(MIRIAM grows silent.)* A star-shaped mole, as I think of it.

MIRIAM. What have you done with my daughter?

VACEK. There was a game we played at the orphanage. I learned it from one of the older girls. We called it "Baptism."

(MIRIAM screams and falls to her knees just as GUNTER walks in the room. He's carrying some clothing for MIRIAM. There's a moment of silence as he takes in the scene.)

GUNTER. Kapo Vacek—they're serving whiskey in the officers' mess. Have you had breakfast yet? *(To MIRIAM as he tosses her a pair of men's pants.)* Put these on. *(He walks around VACEK who covers her breasts with her hands.)* Vacek. My favorite Kapo. Do you ever get bored here at Auschwitz? No, of course not. What a

dumb question that was. Rumor has it you sneak all over
the camp like some dark phantom. You know all the secret little hiding places, don't you? I know this will
sound terribly mundane, but when I get bored, I like to
read personnel files. Yours fascinates me. I read it at
least once a month. *(To MIRIAM.)* If the SS could figure
out how, they'd mass produce this one. When they
brought her here, she was perfect—single, no family, no
loved ones, institutionalized mentality—

MIRIAM. Single? No family? What do you mean? *(To
VACEK.)* Horst? And your son, Anton?

GUNTER. Have you been making up stories again, Eva?
(Silence, then to MIRIAM.) Horst was apparently the
name of the gardener at the convent. He attacked and
raped her the night before she was to give herself to
God. She ran away. The SS found her whoring on street
corners and not long after that she ended up here. And...
(Beat.) Come, come, Eva. You can tell the doctor's wife.

VACEK *(rocking back and forth in the water in the tub;
half-laughing, half-crying).* They said I was inferior.
So—they—fixed—me!

GUNTER *(picks up a towel and tosses it to her).* Get
dressed, you ugly whore. *(Hands MIRIAM a coat and a
cap.)* Put the coat on and pull the cap low over your
eyes.

*(As GUNTER and MIRIAM start to exit, VACEK calls
out to MIRIAM.)*

VACEK. Miriam. Sarah's star-shaped mole—right here—
(She points to a place inside her thigh.) Thank God it
wasn't a Star of David!

(GUNTER and MIRIAM exit.)

SCENE THREE

AT RISE: *Lights come up on JONAH and CANADA in laboratory. On the dissecting table center stage, there is a corpse covered with a sheet. Along the upstage side of the table, there are five metal bowls, each of which contains an organ from the autopsied body. JONAH will weigh and measure the organs throughout the scene. CANADA will take notes.*

JONAH. Who is this? *(Beat.)* Canada, I said—is something wrong?

CANADA. I love working here.

JONAH. You're not serious.

CANADA. There are so few places in this camp where a man can stand in a room and almost hear silence and not be pushed and shoved along with hundreds of other pushing and shoving poor souls.

JONAH. Good. I'm glad you work here. *(JONAH's attitude gets playful.)* I hear there are many openings at the Russian front. A transfer would not be that hard to—

CANADA. I catch cold so easily! Maybe I'd better not.

JONAH. Rommel is short-handed. Can you drive a tank?

CANADA. Much too—too closed in. And all that sand—

JONAH. Some would call it—tropical.

CANADA. Not the right time of year. No. I'd better stay here.

JONAH *(looking around)*. Not much chance for advancement.

CANADA. Believe me. I don't mind going unnoticed!

(They start to laugh and soon they can't control themselves.)

JONAH. Well, as long as you're staying, let's get to work. Who is this?

CANADA. The first of a pair of Gypsy twins, ten years old. I'm ready for your notes, Doctor... Distinguishing marks?

JONAH. Hair color—brown. Eyes—heterochrome—one brown, the other blue.

CANADA. Anything else?

JONAH. Yes, there was a small, pale red spot in his upper arm.

CANADA. Hypodermic needle?

JONAH. I almost missed it.

CANADA. A typhus shot?

JONAH. The subject looked healthy. I can't imagine why he would've required an injection. We'll find out when we examine the organs I've removed... First, I will look at the brain.

(Some moments of silent activity. Outside, the sound of men playing futball *can be heard. This noise will intrude occasionally throughout the scene.)*

JONAH. What is that commotion?

CANADA. The off-duty SS and the Sonderkommando are playing *futball*.

JONAH. *Futball?* How nice. *(He continues with the autopsy.)* What do you think we'd find if we cut this place open?

CANADA. Auschwitz?

JONAH. Something has died here. Some part of humanity that's supposed to be alive. I'd like to strip away the exterior and examine the insides. How can this place exist?

CANADA. Other than the obvious, what answer do you think you'd find?

JONAH. And what is the obvious?

CANADA. The Nazis hate all Jews.

JONAH. The tongue is normal in size and weight for a boy his age.

CANADA. They have no use for us.

JONAH. List this curiosity, please. Under the skin around the neck, just above the upper extremity of the sternum, there was a tumor the size of a small nut. I am now pressing on it with my forceps.

CANADA. Anything?

JONAH. It is filled with a thick pus. Note this in the report: patient has DuBois' tumor.

CANADA. Hereditary syphilis?

JONAH. When I cut it out, I left some healthy tissue around it. Preserve it in formaldehyde.

CANADA. I hate the smell of that.

JONAH. I'm going to examine the lungs... You hate the smell of formaldehyde. My Sarah hates cabbage. A liar hates the truth... Hate takes so many different forms... Tell me, Canada, how does hate become a mass murder?

CANADA. I don't know, Doctor.

JONAH. Not knowing—maybe that's what it is all about.

CANADA. You don't think they know what they're doing?

JONAH. Oh, they do indeed. They're trying to exterminate a race of people. This Gypsy boy. Do you think he had a nickname?

CANADA. I don't know.

JONAH. Exactly. And neither do they. They don't know what he liked most of all in the whole world, or what he was afraid of, or what he enjoyed in school, if he ever went to one. If you multiply this one boy—or any of us—by hundreds of thousands, you have a race of people.

CANADA. Numbers—to be lined up and marched into the gas chamber.

JONAH. Something like that, yes... There is evidence of cavernous tuberculosis. Note that in the report, please.

CANADA. Yes, Doctor... So their hate for us isn't the main reason for Auschwitz?

JONAH. To conquer the world takes either great goodness or great evil. If there weren't any Jews in Europe, the Nazis probably would've invented some. *(He picks up last item from fifth bowl.)* The heart also seems normal in weight and size—the coloring is—what is this?

CANADA. Have you found something?

JONAH. In the exterior coat of the left ventricle, another small, pale red spot.

CANADA. Why a hypodermic injection into the heart?

JONAH. In severe cases of heart failure—

CANADA. He's only ten years old.

JONAH. The blood in the left ventricle—it's coagulated into a compact mass. I smell something. A faint odor.

CANADA. Do you recognize it?

JONAH. Chloroform. This explains the needle mark in the arm. The boy was put to sleep, probably with Evipol, and then chloroform was injected directly into the heart. The blood of the left ventricle coagulated, then deposited itself on the valves—instantaneous death by heart failure. Do not write that down!

CANADA. What should I put for the cause of death?

JONAH. Josef Mengele! ...I'm sorry, I'll fill it in later.

CANADA. He must have known you would find this. What will you put down?

JONAH. I don't know. The truth won't do anyone any good, not now, not here. Damn them! Every breath you take once you've found out what this place is about just sucks you in deeper and deeper.

CANADA. You didn't kill the boy.

(More noise is heard outside. GUNTER comes in to the laboratory, looks around for a moment.)

GUNTER. Is Mengele here?

JONAH. His wife is visiting the camp for a few days. He's taken the afternoon off.

(GUNTER goes off for a moment and comes back on with MIRIAM who looks more like a man than a woman in the clothes he's provided for her. She runs to JONAH when she sees him and they embrace.)

GUNTER *(to CANADA)*. Take her to the doctor's room and be quick about it. Talk to no one and answer no questions if you're stopped. Understand? *(CANADA nods and waits a moment for JONAH and his wife to finish saying hello.)* Now!

(CANADA takes MIRIAM off. GUNTER takes off his uniform coat and starts rolling up his sleeve.)

GUNTER. Once we're done here, you'll have plenty of time to visit with your wife. Your supply shipment? It's all arrived?

JONAH. Yes, Captain. *(Goes to the cabinet and takes out a vial of morphine and then prepares a syringe.)*

GUNTER *(looking at his watch)*. Already three o'clock in the afternoon and I still have another full day's work ahead of me. Trains coming and going on into the night... God, it just never ends. And now Captain Rhodes—he's come down with—did you see him earlier?

JONAH *(filling the syringes)*. He has a fever of a hundred and one, nausea—I sent him to bed.

GUNTER. Thanks to him I'm stuck with ramp duty this evening. Two more trains scheduled to arrive. God only knows when I'll get to have dinner. And then another train leaving at nine.

(JONAH brings over the syringe and sets it on the desk next to GUNTER. GUNTER picks it up and examines it for a moment.)

GUNTER. I'm curious, Doctor. Do you think I'm weak because of this?

JONAH *(putting away the supplies)*. Who can judge another man's pain?

GUNTER *(gives himself the injection of morphine)*. I suppose you consider yourself an expert on pain.

JONAH *(pointing to the dead boy on the autopsy table)*. Why don't you ask him about pain. *(Throughout the following, JONAH cleans up after the autopsy—washes instruments in a pan of soapy water, etc.)*

GUNTER. One of Mengele's twins? *(JONAH nods.)* He has a whole barracks filled with them. They call it "the zoo."

JONAH. Is my daughter all right?

GUNTER. As far as I know. You can ask your wife when—

JONAH. How long will I get to see her today?

GUNTER *(reaching into his uniform coat pocket, taking out a slip of paper which he leaves on the desk)*. I've written out a pass for you to go back and forth to see your wife—and your daughter too. Save me the trouble of bringing her back and forth every time. Take an hour maybe and then see that she gets back to the women's section.

JONAH. Thank you.

GUNTER. I'm a reasonable man.

JONAH. I never thought anything else.

GUNTER. Go to hell, you stupid Jew! *(Beat.)* If you could trade places with me—would you? *(No answer from JONAH.)* I'll tell you what, Doctor. You be with me tonight on the train ramp when the cars come in filled with your kind. I'll let you help me decide who lives and who dies!

JONAH. No one would allow that—a Jew watching trainloads of people going—

GUNTER. Why? What would you do?

JONAH. I might yell—scream out at them—tell them what they're walking into! You'd have a huge revolt on your hands.

GUNTER *(laughing uproariously).* Who do you think would believe you? Society molds people to conform. Obey the law, obey anybody with a uniform and a badge of office, a holster, a pistol. Who can go against authority like that? You, me, the people on the trains— *(He shakes his head meaning none of them could do it.)* None of us! The world just doesn't work that way.

JONAH. So if one policeman, or a thousand tell you to violate what you know to be right—you'll go ahead and do it?

GUNTER. What I know to be right? Who taught me that? Those thousand policeman with their uniforms and their badges and their guns!

JONAH. What about your head, and your heart, and your mind—don't they tell you anything?

GUNTER. Be on the ramp tonight at seven o'clock—that's an order—and I'll show you what they tell me.

(Lights go down as waltz music is heard.)

SCENE FOUR

SCENE: *JONAH's room center stage.*

AT RISE: *When JONAH enters, MIRIAM is cutting LENA's hair so she'll resemble all the rest of the women in the camp. CANADA is using a hypodermic syringe to*

put a tattoo on LENA's arm. JONAH crosses to MIRIAM
and leans down and gives her a kiss hello.

JONAH. What can I do to help?

CANADA *(pointing to a flimsy coat on the end of the bed)*.
See that coat there? I've torn the hem at the bottom.
Take these coins and sew them into the lining. *(He takes
coins from his pocket and hands them to JONAH.)*

JONAH. These are gold!

CANADA. She might need them along the way.

(JONAH gets a needle and thread and starts to work.)

LENA. How do you like my new haircut, Dr. Jonah?

MIRIAM. I'm sorry. My scissors aren't very sharp and I'm
not much of a barber.

JONAH. You look beautiful. *(To CANADA.)* So what is
your plan?

CANADA. First we have to somehow get Lena into the
women's camp.

MIRIAM. The two hundred women going north on tonight's train will leave through the west gate.

JONAH. Can't she join them when they're on the train
ramp?

CANADA. That's much too risky. I'd rather she be with
the group when they leave for the train. But I'm still not
sure how we're going to get her in there.

JONAH. It sounds like we've failed before we've begun.

MIRIAM. Isaac! Watch your tongue.

CANADA. Remember the corpse brought in this morning?
The woman with no clothes, red hair— Mengele wants
an autopsy when we can get around to it—

JONAH. Probably a stroke victim—although we won't know until we—

MIRIAM. She died last night. We shared a bunk. She was from Budapest too. She'd been here two months. She'd been selected for tonight's train. She was talking about how lucky she was that she was leaving. She was holding my hand and suddenly stopped talking, coughed once or twice; her hand on mine grew terribly tight—and she died.

JONAH. What did you do?

MIRIAM. I fought off the others and I took her clothes for Sarah.

CANADA. Where are the clothes now?

MIRIAM. I made Sarah put them on under her uniform. I was thinking of what you told my husband about the winter.

CANADA (to JONAH). Since you didn't perform the autopsy yet, you've issued no death certificate, right? (JONAH nods.) Then her number will still be on the list of prisoners leaving on that train tonight. And it's her number I'm tattooing on Lena's arm.

MIRIAM. And Sarah has her uniform.

LENA (looking at her arm). Will that come off.

CANADA. Not for a while. It's just water and India ink. I'm sorry if this hurts but I've got to pierce the skin to make your tattoo number.

LENA. Do the numbers mean anything?

CANADA. The digits tell the train you were on, the country and the city or town you came from. Tonight you'll have to show this to the officer on duty. It will be dark, but there are always lights on the train ramp. You'll be

with many other women. Don't look anyone in the eye.
Walk slow and stare straight ahead of you.

JONAH. I'm going to be on the train ramp tonight.

CANADA. Why?

JONAH. Captain Gunter ordered me to accompany him.
Some lesson he wants to teach me; I don't know.

CANADA. Gunter has train duty this evening? He's seen
Lena! Remember? Here in your room the other night!

JONAH. That's right. He was here. But remember—he was
drunk and she was lying down on the bed, covered with
the blanket. I doubt that he got that good of a look at
her.

CANADA. Did you give him his morphine?

JONAH. Yes. *(To MIRIAM.)* He gave me a pass—to come
and see you and Sarah. Maybe I'll be able to sneak over
some food when I—

CANADA. He gave you a pass? Let me see it! *(JONAH
shows it to CANADA who reads it and gets very excited.)* I think this is it! This is how we'll get Lena into
the women's camp.

MIRIAM. How?

CANADA. This pass is for you. *(He points to JONAH.)* To
get in to see your wife and daughter. What if you accompany your wife *(He points to MIRIAM.)* and your
daughter *(He points to LENA.)* to the gate, with this—
and maybe a little bribe—I bet it'll work. The pass is for
you going in—it'll work for you getting them back in,
too! I'm certain of it!

MIRIAM. What kind of bribe? And why?

CANADA. Something to distract the guard. They'd all sell
you Hitler's moustache for the right amount of gold,
but—

JONAH. What about some of these coins?

CANADA. I was really hoping they'd be for later on down the road.

LENA *(reaching in to her pocket for her mother's ring)*. Use this. *(She hands it to CANADA.)*

CANADA. Are you sure?

LENA. Yes.

(CANADA puts ring in his shirt pocket. MIRIAM's done with LENA's hair. She goes to the window. JONAH sees that she's bothered by something and goes to her and puts his arms around her. They kiss. Behind them CANADA is showing LENA a portion of a map.)

MIRIAM. That Kapo woman. She told the most vicious lies about you.

JONAH. Let me guess. Something about another woman. *(By the look on MIRIAM's face he can see he is right.)* You didn't believe her, I hope.

MIRIAM *(looking around Jonah's room)*. She made it sound like you had hundreds of dancing girls in here.

JONAH *(looks around and then shows size with thumb and index finger)*. They were very tiny. *(They both laugh, but then MIRIAM's laughter turns into tears.)* What's wrong?

MIRIAM. Why can't our Sarah go?

JONAH. I know. I know. I've been asking myself the same thing for—

MIRIAM. It might be the difference between life and death.

JONAH. And here we are helping someone else's child stay alive.

MIRIAM. Isaac, there's something I have to tell you.

JONAH. What is it, Miriam?

MIRIAM. I've been your wife long enough to know what you believe in. I know the great value you put on life. I've given a lot of thought to this. I want you to know— if things get bad for Sarah—and me—really get bad— *(JONAH turns away from her.)* Look at me, Isaac. Look in my eyes. If things get—worse than you can ever imagine for Sarah—or for me—I will take matters into my own hands.

JONAH. No! Miriam, no! Please. You can't give up!

MIRIAM. I'm not giving up, Isaac. Giving up is easy. I'm just facing the truth.

JONAH. What's wrong is wrong. *(She turns away from him, discouraged.)* I don't know what kind of truth could be so horrible that you would—

MIRIAM. Of course you don't, Isaac. And I don't want you to! Ever! *(She kisses him and returns to LENA and CANADA.)*

CANADA *(showing her small piece of map he's copied).* Lena, this is where you are now. And this is where the train is heading. If you can escape, head east, in this direction, towards the Russian border. The best time to try to escape is after your train arrives but before you get to the camp. There may be confusion, a truck breakdown or something. Try to use that. But don't wait too long. If you're in the new camp three, four, five days—a routine sets in and the chances to get out grow less and less.

JONAH. Escape? What are you talking about? Getting out of here and to a work camp—isn't that enough? Why this dangerous talk of escaping yet again?

CANADA *(to LENA).* I know I'm asking an awful lot of you, Lena. From everything we know, the war isn't going well for the Germans. Who knows how much time we have left here.

MIRIAM. That's good news!

CANADA. Maybe not. *(To all of them as he takes ring from his shirt pocket.)* Do you really think the Nazis will walk away from these camps leaving all of us alive to testify to the world about what went on here? *(To LENA.)* If you can, Lena—escape—tell someone about your mother, *(He gestures with the ring.)* about your father. The world has to know and we may not have much time left. *(He returns ring to his shirt pocket.)* Are you almost done with the lining, Doctor?

JONAH. Just finishing. Lena, I'll be on the train ramp this evening, so look for me. I doubt that we'll be able to talk, but I'll be there. And I'll be praying for you.

CANADA *(to JONAH).* When you leave for the ramp, take me with you. Before Gunter sees me, I'll slip in with the crew unloading the baggage. *(To LENA.)* Dr. Jonah's been sewing some pieces of gold in to the lining of your coat. Use that if you need to pay someone for help.

JONAH. Remember, your getting out of here is the most important thing. If you can escape once you're clear of this place—fine. But be careful, don't take any crazy risks.

LENA. Yes, Doctor.

JONAH. And, Lena, if things get bad and you're afraid—just close your eyes and sing. Maybe quietly, just to yourself—but sing. That will give you courage. Will you do that?

LENA. You are so much like my poppa.

CANADA. All right. Is there anything we've missed or forgotten?

LENA. Could we say the *Shema* together?

(They all nod their heads and say the prayer with her.)

ALL. Hear O Israel, the Lord is our God, the Lord is one. Blessed is the name of his glorious majesty, forever and ever. Love the Lord your God with all—

(VACEK enters.)

VACEK. Welcome to Synagogue Auschwitz! *(Silence as they stare at her.)* Well, well! Canada, it's your young friend from last night, the one who masquerades as Jonah's daughter. What exactly did I interrupt? Is that why I was attacked from behind? You saw who drugged me! Tell me who it was!

CANADA. I don't know what you're talking about.

VACEK *(to JONAH)*. Whoever she is, she is not supposed to be in your room and she is in real danger, Jew doctor—unless you convince your friend here to— *(She finally notices MIRIAM who's had her back to VACEK.)* What's she doing here? *(No one answers her.)* This is a very strange gathering, Doctor. *(She thinks of something.)* Escape! Is that what you're planning??

JONAH. Kapo Vacek, please, if you'd just listen—

VACEK. Because of what happened last night, I'm no longer the Kapo for the women's hospital. You and somebody else drugged me and threw me to the wolves. But you don't have to tell me a thing, Canada. When Gunter sees this—along with the butcher Mengele, I'll get my job back quicker than you three can go up the chimney! Did you hear me, Jacob Tannenbaum? *(She pushes his chest.)* When I get through here tonight, you'll all be dead! *(She feels inside his shirt pocket and removes LENA's mother's ring.)* Oh, I like this. Thank you! *(She grabs LENA's hand and starts to pull her off.)* You're mine now.

MIRIAM. The hell she is, you bitch!

(VACEK turns and runs into MIRIAM's scissors. She doubles over as MIRIAM pushes them deep into her stomach. MIRIAM almost picks VACEK up in the air as she drives the scissors further and further into her. Finally, she lets go of the scissors and VACEK falls to the floor. They all stare in silence.)

LENA. Is she—dead?

JONAH *(kneels and feels for a pulse)*. Yes, she is.

MIRIAM. I'm so sorry. I don't know what came over me but—everything just— *(She begins to cry as JONAH puts his arms around her.)*

JONAH. It's all right, Miriam. Don't cry. I love you!

CANADA. We have to do something with this body. *(To JONAH.)* Did Gunter say anything about trains arriving tonight?

JONAH *(nodding)*. Two. Before Lena's train leaves.

CANADA. That means later tonight— *(Closes his eyes at the horror.)* There'll be hundreds and hundreds of dead bodies to burn. If somehow we could get her from here—

JONAH. Too risky! *(He thinks of something.)* Wait a moment. Mengele's shipment of specimens going to Berlin.

CANADA. The body parts?

JONAH. Not all the specimen bottles are full.

CANADA. My God, Dr. Moses. You are really getting good at this!

(LENA crosses to VACEK's body, takes her mother's ring from VACEK's pocket and hands it to MIRIAM who hugs her in return.)

JONAH. Come, Lena. It's time to get you free of this place!

(They exit, spirits elevated and confident. Lights go down. Waltz music is heard.)

SCENE FIVE

SCENE: *Train ramp.*

AT RISE: *It is evening and getting dark. GUNTER and JONAH on ramp, GUNTER selecting, JONAH observing. GUNTER holds a clipboard and he is also directing crew unloading baggage. Upstage, perhaps on scrim, we see two lines of shadows, most going left, some right. Intermixed are sound of trucks departing and far-off waltz music from camp orchestra.*

GUNTER. You—left. *Link. Link.* You, over there, *recht—* to the right. *Link. Link.* Yes, madam, by all means keep your child with you; go to the left there. *Link. Link. Link.*

to SR

JONAH *(aside)*. Ask her the child's name. How old is she? Is that her favorite doll she's carrying?

GUNTER. At the end of my first year as manager at my firm, profits had grown one and a half percent, a fair showing, I thought... You, to the right, *recht!* Yes. The rest of you, on the left, please... But the owner said he hadn't promoted me to manager just to achieve fair results.

JONAH. What did you do?   *Back SR*

GUNTER *(to unseen workers)*. Get those cars unloaded! *Mach schnell!* Start piling up everything out here for the trucks to pick up. Move! Move! *(To JONAH.)* I fiddled with our packaging systems and the delivery process. I achieved only marginal results. The actual manufacturing of the product was precise—there was nothing I could touch in that area. Then I began to look at our staff. *(Returning attention to lines of prisoners.)* Left. Left. Quickly! *Zwillinge!* If any of you are twins, report here, now!

back

enter (SL)

(CANADA comes on wearing a cap low over his head. He carries two or three suitcases. He drops one and it opens. He rifles through contents, putting some things in his pockets, as he feels lining of clothes, tests the heels of shoes etc.)   *d Stage (R)*

GUNTER. I soon realized that once a new employee mastered his job—usually within a month or two, there was little or no difference between his output and that of employees who'd been with the firm for twenty years.

JONAH. Was this your answer?

GUNTER. I fired the ten most senior employees and replaced them with new hires whose salaries equaled that of two of the ten I'd just let go. Within six months, we'd increased profits by another two percentage points. *(Returning his attention to the prisoners.) Link. Link.* You also please, to the left. Any questions, Doctor?

JONAH *(aside).* Ask that old grandfather down there if he still dreams of making love. Ask him if he reads the Bible and takes his children fishing.

GUNTER *(spotting CANADA loafing).* You're not out here on holiday! Get a move on. *Schnell! Schnell!*

(CANADA goes off for more luggage.)

JONAH. So the lesson you wanted to teach me—

GUNTER. Is right in front of you. The right and wrong of this world we establish, day in and day out—

JONAH. In a concentration camp? In the middle of a war?

GUNTER. What is "war," Doctor? It's business! It always has been. Even when you mask it behind revenge or right versus wrong or territorial expansion—at the heart of it all is business! Profits and losses.

JONAH. All these people you send to their death—

GUNTER. My ten colleagues with the most seniority—I never heard anything about them after they left. I presume they survived; I don't know. It wasn't my job to know; I did my job. The sky did not come crashing down. Look around you, Doctor. Do you see the sky falling anywhere? *(No response from JONAH.)* This next group of ten, Doctor. *Link?* Or *recht?*

JONAH *(automatically). Recht—recht—recht—*

GUNTER *(to unseen people).* Halt! All of you—halt! *(To JONAH.)* What are you doing? The old man with the beard. Why should Germany spend money to keep him alive?

JONAH. Think of the stories he could tell the children!

GUNTER. I keep no children! I tell no stories! This is business, Doctor—not some fairy tale! *(To the people.)* All of you—link! Link! To the left! *(To JONAH.)* Somehow I knew this lesson would be lost on you. Stand aside, Doctor.

(JONAH steps to the back. CANADA comes back on with an old steamer trunk. GUNTER yells to offstage left where women await boarding.)

GUNTER. Get those women ready for boarding the train. *(CANADA exits for more baggage.)* Attention! Line up in single file and as you pass this point— *(He indicates area in front of where he's standing.)* Show me your number. *(He points offstage to first in the unseen line of women.)* Over here now. Let's go! *Schnell!*

(As GUNTER looks and then checks off numbers on his list, the women come on stage. We only see LENA, fifth or sixth in line. She takes one step forward, stops, waits for line to move, then another step and so on as they pass in front of GUNTER. She looks around her, trying not to make eye contact with anyone. She is hunched over, shoulders drooping, trying to hide within herself. She is obviously frightened.)

GUNTER. Get on that car there and fill it completely until I order you to start on the next one.

start humming

(We can see LENA's lips begin to move as she sings to herself.)

JONAH *(aside).* You can do it, Lena. That's right. Just move with the line, just another number going on the train.

LENA *(frightened, says some of the words to* "Roshenkis Mit Mandlen"*).* "...Mother her watch will keep, to bring you back— *(Her voice cracking, she softly sings the rest of the words.)* raisins and almonds, Sleep my little one, sleep."

sing

(We can see that GUNTER hears her singing.)

GUNTER. Have your sleeves rolled up and keep the line moving!

(LENA is next. CANADA sees this as he comes on with more luggage. LENA stops in front of GUNTER and holds out her arm to show him her number. She is nervous and her arm is shaking. GUNTER grabs her arm to steady it, reads the number, and crosses one off his list. CANADA sees all this and drops suitcases to distract GUNTER who then yells at CANADA.)

target yells him

GUNTER. Be careful with that, you dumb bastard! Get the hell out of here if you can't do the job right! Get on back to your block! *(CANADA exits.)* Keep the line moving! Let's go! *Schnell!*

Canada exit SR

(He looks at the retreating figure of CANADA, then over at LENA—we see him start to put two and two together. He crosses to LENA, grabs her arm, spits on her arm and then rubs at the tattoo and sees that it was a fake.)

GUNTER. That was a beautiful lullaby, little girl. Sit over there and don't move!

that Canada has pulled out.

(LENA sits on steamer trunk. JONAH comes forward.)

Stop him, physically

→ start towards her.

GUNTER. Is she your daughter?

JONAH. What difference does it make?

GUNTER. Answer my question!

JONAH. She might as well be.

GUNTER. Who is she?

JONAH. She is no one. She doesn't exist anywhere, on any records. Please, Captain Gunter—one more person, in this camp or out of this camp—it can't make a difference. Please! I'm begging you! Let her go!

GUNTER. You know I can't do that. *→ look down*

JONAH. What?

GUNTER. *Link.* The line on the left. She has to go with them.

animated

JONAH. She's been through that—yesterday! The whole thing: the speech, the lies, the undressing, the crowded gas chamber—her mother, her father—all of them naked, helpless, frightened. She has smelled the gas, Gunter! And I don't know why—maybe God wanted it that way—but somehow, she lived! She survived! You can't make her go through that again! Even a Jew shouldn't have to die twice in one lifetime!!

GUNTER *(reaching for his side arm).* Then I will take care of it.

JONAH. What do you mean?

GUNTER. I'm sorry, Doctor. It has to be. What you say about yesterday—maybe God did want it that way. But today is today, and this is the way God wants it today.

JONAH. Whose God?

GUNTER. Mine!

JONAH. Which God is that? The one you pump into your arm?

⟶ to his head.

GUNTER *(gun out of the holster).* Are you threatening me?

JONAH. I—don't—know.

GUNTER. Good.

JONAH. But you said if I did something for you, you could help me.

GUNTER. Not in this case.

JONAH. She's only sixteen years old! Her name is—

getting
him.

GUNTER *(reaches out, puts his hand over JONAH's mouth).* I don't want to know! Now stand aside, Doctor. *(GUNTER takes a step toward LENA.)*

JONAH. Wait! *(GUNTER looks back at JONAH. JONAH closes his eyes and then decides.)* She knows me. She trusts me.

(Realizing what JONAH is suggesting, GUNTER looks in his face trying to decide if he can trust him.)

GUNTER. All right. But first, look around you: rifles, side arms, at least ten machine guns! All I have to do is raise my arm, point to the side of your head and give one shout. Don't do anything foolish, Doctor.

(JONAH nods. GUNTER drops his side arm into pocket of JONAH's lab coat. JONAH crosses, stands behind trunk LENA is sitting on. Lights go down. Spotlight on just the two of them.)

go behind Lena

JONAH. How are you, Lena?

LENA. It didn't work, did it?

JONAH. No, it didn't. I'm sorry.

LENA. Are they going to kill me?

JONAH. No. They are not.

LENA. What's going to happen to me?

JONAH. Would you mind staying here—with me?

LENA. I'm scared.

JONAH. There's nothing to be scared of, believe me. We're going to take care of you, like a family. You have me and you have Canada and Miriam, and don't forget Sarah. You're going to be fine. All right?

hand — on shoulder

LENA. All right, Doctor.

JONAH. Call me Isaac. — Sit by her—facing backward

LENA. In the Hebrew, Isaac means "laughter."

JONAH. Yes, that's right. I'd forgotten that. Isaac—laughter. Then we should laugh, shouldn't we? Let's laugh and sing!

LENA. What's there to laugh about?

JONAH. Have you seen your haircut? And the dirt smudged on your face? *(He tries to laugh.)* And what about me? Look at the stitches in your coat! Miriam always said I was good maybe at cutting things open but I sure couldn't sew them up. *(He tries to laugh again.)* You know what I think, Lena? Beautiful things like laughter and singing—they're God's gift to us. They're inside of you. No one can steal them away. So when we laugh and sing, it's like we're praying the best prayers we can because we're giving God's gift back to him. When you laugh and sing, Lena—inside you are free! Would you sing for me, please?

LENA. Here? Now?

JONAH. Yes. Why not? Sing your favorite song for me, Lena. Sing happy!!

Jonah stand

(LENA sings, hesitantly at first, saying the words more than singing. As the sound of her own voice gives her courage, she sings louder.)

LENA. "My *dreidel*'s always playful, it loves to dance and spin. A happy game of *dreidel*, So come now let's begin." *(JONAH leans forward so gun in his pocket is right behind her head.)* Oh *dreidel, dreidel*, it loves to dance and spin, Oh *dreidel, dreidel, dreidel*, so come now let's begin."

(JONAH pulls the trigger. There's a loud gunshot. Her head jerks back and JONAH comes around the side of the trunk, catches her, and sits holding her in his arms. He closes her sightless eyes.)

hold her
sing her lullaby

JONAH. "Oh *dreidel, dreidel, dreidel*."

(As with LENA, the sound of his own voice gives him courage and as he recites the lines to the song, he gets louder. JONAH realizes at one and the same time, the tragedy of this moment but also, a kind of triumph. The courage he's found inside himself to change his beliefs is

*the same quiet courage that has helped Jews survive op-
pression for centuries.)*

GUNTER *(offstage voice)*. *Link!*
JONAH. "A leg so short and thin."
GUNTER *(offstage voice)*. *Recht!*
JONAH. "Oh *dreidel, dreidel, dreidel—*"
GUNTER *(offstage voice)*. *Link!*
JONAH. "It drops—and then I win."

(Lights; curtain.)

END OF PLAY

PRODUCTION NOTES

Although *Auschwitz Lullaby* was originally written to be performed in smaller, more intimate performance spaces, I have seen it done in 70-seat theatres as well as 550-seat thrust stage auditoriums. It can work well in both spaces as long as the production is imaginative and suggestive rather than one hundred percent realistic. The amount of dialogue seems to better fit a suggestive motif rather than a literally realistic one.

While the staging should be suggestive, the costuming should be as realistic as possible. The inmates' uniforms must be historically accurate as well as worn, dirty, and probably uncomfortable. Captain Gunter's uniform must be accurate and his side arm should be a German luger.

The nudity in Scene Two, Act One in the gas chamber can be handled in a number of different ways running the gamut from none to complete. When Jonah and Canada come on, Canada is carrying a blanket and he immediately covers Lena who, historically speaking, like all the bodies in the gas chamber, should be naked. The actress can be naked, she can wear a body stocking, or she might even have on bra and panties. She should be in very little light off to the side so this shouldn't be that big of a problem. The "lattice-work sculpture" of intertwined bodies in the background representing the gassed people can also be handled a number of different ways. Nudity, body stockings, half light to almost no light at all, and a scrim with a one-dimensional representation of this "mountain" are perfectly acceptable.

In Scene Two of Act Two, Miriam gives Kapo Vacek a sponge bath. This also can involve nudity but it has been performed with Vacek wearing a sleeveless tank top or T-shirt. If the water is suggested with the use of a pitcher and a sponge, then Vacek being slightly dressed is not usually a problem for the audience. Vacek should be sitting in a half tub, something that is portable and would show us her legs sticking out the front from the knees on down.

The language of the play should not be too much of a problem. The swearing has been kept to a minimum in favor of more intense language. If "bitch" and "damn" are a problem for younger audiences, directors should feel free to substitute other words.

Miriam's hair can actually be cut for the performances or she can wear a short babushka type of cloth over her head as many women prisoners did and just suggest the loss of hair.

The laughter in parts of the play should be as realistic as possible. There was much laughter—albeit macabre—in the camps.

After the gunshot at the end of the play, Jonah should try to move as quickly as possible around to the front of the steamer trunk Lena has been sitting on so that he can catch her and prevent her body from falling to the floor. He sits and holds her as the play ends. The effect should be reminiscent of Michelangelo's *Pietà*.

ADDITIONAL CHARACTER DESCRIPTIONS

DR. ISAAC JONAH: He is an intellectual rather than a physical man. As a doctor, he believes in the sanctity of life. Because he works for Mengele, he wears regular street clothes covered by a white lab coat.

JACOB "CANADA" TANNENBAUM: He is quiet, looks bookish but is an expert organizer—he finds things to use in the camp in order to survive. His uniform has a yellow Star of David until he starts working for Mengele.

CAPTAIN HANS GUNTER: Not really a soldier, Gunter looks at the war as an opportunity to advance his career. He lost full use of an arm in an industrial accident before the war.

KAPO EVA VACEK: She is in charge of the prisoners working in the women's hospital. Vacek is average: height, weight, and looks. Vacek is sadistic and is jealous of anything having to do with family life. She wears a green star, unlike the Jewish yellow. Although she wears a prisoner uniform, because she is a Kapo she is allowed to personalize hers with boots or vest or hat.

MIRIAM JONAH: She is a wife and mother used to her somewhat upper-class position in society. Her uniform will have a yellow Star of David.

LENA: She is from Budapest, is bright, and likes music and singing.

Roshenkis Mit Mandlen

(Raisins and Almonds)

Arranged by
JOSEPH M. ESTELLA

Words and Music by
ABR. GOLDFADDEN

DIRECTOR'S NOTES